CONNECT AND CONVERT

MAXIMIZING YOUR SOCIAL MEDIA REACH THROUGH CONTENT MARKETING

DS VIGNESH

Made with ♥ on the Notion Press Platform
www.notionpress.com

Contents

Contents

CHAPTER ONE

About the Author

I'm pleased to introduce the my self as a author of this book, Ds Vignesh. As a digital marketing professional, I has a wealth of experience in helping small and medium businesses grow their online visibility and traffic. I have worked with a variety of companies, providing guidance and expertise to help them succeed in the competitive world of online marketing.

With this book, “Connect and Convert: Maximizing Your Social Media Reach through Content Marketing”, I shared my knowledge and expertise on how to effectively use content marketing to reach and engage with your target audience on social media. I have provides clear explanations and practical tips on how to develop a successful content marketing strategy, so you can grow your online visibility, increase your traffic, and ultimately drive conversions.

Whether you are a small business owner, marketer, or digital professional, “Connect and Convert” is a must-read for anyone looking to take their content marketing efforts to the next level. With its practical advice and insider tips, this book is the ultimate guide to maximizing your social media reach through content marketing. So sit back, relax, and get ready to learn from the expert, Ds Vignesh.

CHAPTER TWO

Introduction: The Importance of Content Marketing in Social Media

Social media has become an integral part of our daily lives and has drastically changed the way we communicate and consume information. As a result, it has become an important platform for businesses to connect with their target audience and promote their brand. Content marketing, the creation and sharing of valuable, relevant, and consistent content, is a critical component of a successful social media marketing strategy.

The Importance of Content Marketing in Social Media

Building Brand Awareness: Social media provides businesses with the opportunity to reach a large, targeted audience and increase brand awareness. By consistently creating and sharing valuable content, businesses can engage with their target audience, build brand loyalty, and position themselves as industry leaders.

Driving Traffic and Lead Generation: Effective content marketing can drive traffic to your website and increase lead generation. By creating content that solves a problem, provides value, or inspires action, you can attract and retain visitors, convert them into leads, and ultimately drive sales.

Improving Customer Engagement: Content marketing helps businesses build relationships with their target audience and improve customer engagement. By creating content that is relevant, valuable, and consistent, businesses can engage with their audience, respond to their needs, and foster long-term customer relationships.

Establishing Thought Leadership: Content marketing provides businesses with the opportunity to establish thought leadership and position themselves as experts in their industry. By consistently creating and sharing industry-related content, businesses can demonstrate their knowledge and expertise, establish their credibility, and differentiate themselves from their competition.

Cost-Effective Marketing: Compared to traditional advertising methods, content marketing is a cost-effective way to reach and engage with your target audience. By creating and sharing valuable content, businesses can establish and maintain a strong online presence, build brand awareness, and drive business results without the high costs associated with traditional advertising.

The Power of Social Media for Content Marketing

Social media provides businesses with the opportunity to reach a large, targeted audience and promote their brand. With over 4.2 billion active users globally, social media provides businesses with the reach and engagement they need to achieve their marketing goals.

In addition, social media algorithms prioritize content that engages and resonates with users, making it easier for businesses to reach their target audience. By creating and sharing valuable, relevant, and consistent content, businesses can increase brand awareness, drive traffic and lead generation, improve customer engagement, establish thought leadership, and achieve their marketing goals.

In this book, we'll explore the basics of social media content marketing and provide tips on how to effectively create and share content that engages and resonates with your target audience. Whether you're a seasoned marketer or just starting out, this book will provide you with the insights and strategies you need to take your content marketing to the next level.

Content marketing is a critical component of a successful social media marketing strategy. With its ability to build brand awareness, drive traffic and lead generation, improve customer engagement, establish thought leadership, and achieve marketing goals, it's no wonder that content marketing has become a top priority for businesses of all sizes. So, let's dive into the world of social media content marketing and learn how to effectively create and share content that drives results!

CHAPTER THREE

Chapter 1: Defining Content Marketing

Content marketing is a marketing strategy that involves creating and sharing valuable, relevant, and consistent content to attract and retain a clearly defined audience, and ultimately drive profitable customer action. This approach to marketing is all about creating a relationship with your target audience and providing them with information and resources that help them achieve their goals and solve their problems.

In this chapter, we'll explore the history and evolution of content marketing, and why it's become a critical component of any marketing strategy in today's digital age. We'll also discuss the key principles of content marketing and why it's an effective way to build your brand and reach your target audience.

The Benefits of Content Marketing

One of the main benefits of content marketing is that it allows you to build trust and credibility with your target audience by providing them with valuable, informative, and educational content. This helps you establish yourself as an authority in your industry and fosters a sense of loyalty and engagement with your brand.

Another key benefit of content marketing is that it allows you to reach your target audience where they are, whether that's on social media, in search engines, or on your website. By creating and sharing content that is optimized for the channels and platforms where your target audience is active, you can increase your visibility and reach, and ultimately drive more traffic and leads to your business.

Finally, content marketing is an effective way to achieve your business goals, whether that's increasing sales, building brand awareness, or driving engagement. By creating content that aligns with your business goals and resonates with your target audience, you can generate results and demonstrate the value of your content marketing efforts.

The Key Principles of Content Marketing

To be successful with content marketing, it's important to understand the key principles that drive this approach to marketing. These include:

Creating valuable and relevant content: The first and most important principle of content marketing is creating content that is valuable and relevant to your target audience. This means understanding what your audience wants and needs, and creating content that meets those needs and helps them achieve their goals.

Building relationships: Content marketing is all about building relationships with your target audience. This means creating content that is engaging, informative, and educational, and that fosters a sense of community and connection with your brand.

Consistency: Consistency is key when it comes to content marketing. This means creating and sharing content on a regular basis, so that your target audience knows what to expect from your brand and continues to engage with your content.

Measuring success: Finally, it's important to measure the success of your content marketing efforts so that you can continually optimize and improve your strategy. This means setting clear goals, tracking key metrics, and analyzing your results to see what's working and what's not.

Content marketing is a critical component of any marketing strategy in today's digital age. By creating valuable, relevant, and consistent content and building relationships with your target audience, you can increase your visibility, reach, and engagement, and ultimately drive profitable customer action. In the following chapters, we'll dive deeper into the various platforms and channels for content marketing and discuss how to create effective and engaging content marketing campaigns on social media.

CHAPTER FOUR

Chapter 2: Understanding Your Target Audience

Before you begin your content marketing efforts, it's critical to have a deep understanding of your target audience. This includes understanding who they are, what they want, what motivates them, and what their pain points are.

By understanding your target audience, you'll be better equipped to create content that resonates with them and meets their needs. This, in turn, will help you build stronger relationships with your audience and increase the effectiveness of your content marketing efforts.

In this chapter, we'll discuss how to research and understand your target audience, and why this information is so crucial to your content marketing success.

Steps for Understanding Your Target Audience

To get started, follow these steps to research and understand your target audience:

Identify your target audience: Start by defining who your target audience is. This includes demographic information such as age, gender, location, and income, as well as psychographic information such as interests, values, and beliefs.

Conduct market research: Market research is a key part of understanding your target audience. This can involve online surveys, focus groups, or secondary research such as industry reports and data analysis.

Study your customer data: If you have existing customers, studying their data can provide valuable insights into your target audience. This can include information such as purchasing patterns, customer feedback, and demographics.

Engage with your target audience: Engaging directly with your target audience is another important way to understand who they are and what they want. This can involve attending industry events, reaching out to customers for feedback, or engaging in social media.

Analyze your competition: Finally, studying your competition can provide valuable insights into your target audience and what they're looking for. This can include analyzing their content, products, and marketing strategies.

Why Understanding Your Target Audience Matters

Understanding your target audience is crucial to your content marketing success for several reasons:

It helps you create content that resonates with your audience: When you have a deep understanding of your target audience, you'll be better equipped to create content that meets their needs and resonates with them. This, in turn, will help you build stronger relationships with your audience and increase engagement with your content.

It helps you reach your audience where they are: By understanding your target audience, you'll know where they are active and what channels and platforms they use. This, in turn, will help you reach your audience where they are and increase your visibility and reach.

It helps you achieve your business goals: Finally, understanding your target audience is critical to achieving your business goals. By creating content that aligns with your audience's needs and interests, you'll be better equipped to drive the results you're looking for, whether that's increased sales, brand awareness, or engagement.

Understanding your target audience is a critical first step in your content marketing efforts. By conducting research, engaging with your audience, and analyzing your competition, you'll be better equipped to create content that resonates with your target audience and meets their needs. In the following chapters, we'll dive deeper into the various platforms and channels for content marketing and discuss how to create effective and engaging content marketing campaigns on social media.

CHAPTER FIVE

Chapter 3: Creating a Strong Content Marketing Strategy

Now that you have a deep understanding of your target audience, it's time to develop a content marketing strategy. A content marketing strategy is a plan for creating, publishing, and distributing content that meets your target audience's needs and helps you achieve your business goals.

In this chapter, we'll discuss how to create a content marketing strategy that aligns with your business goals and resonates with your target audience.

Steps for Creating a Strong Content Marketing Strategy

Define your business goals: Before you begin, it's important to clearly define your business goals. This could be anything from increasing brand awareness, to driving traffic to your website, to generating leads, to increasing sales.

Determine your target audience's pain points and needs: Based on your research, determine what your target audience's pain points and needs are. This information will inform the type of content you create and the channels you use to distribute it.

Choose the right channels for your audience: Based on your research and understanding of your target audience, choose the channels and platforms that are most appropriate for your target audience. This could include social media platforms, email, or your website.

Define your content themes: Based on your target audience's needs and your business goals, define the content themes you'll be creating. This could be anything from how-to guides and product demos to blog posts and infographics.

Determine your content format: Decide on the format you'll use for your content. This could include blog posts, videos, infographics, or podcasts.

Create a content calendar: Plan out your content in advance using a content calendar. This will help you stay organized and ensure that you're consistently publishing content that meets your target audience's needs and supports your business goals.

Measure and adjust: Finally, measure the effectiveness of your content marketing strategy by tracking your results. Based on your results, adjust your strategy as needed to ensure that you're achieving your business goals and resonating with your target audience.

Why a Strong Content Marketing Strategy Matters

A strong content marketing strategy is critical to your content marketing success for several reasons:

It helps you focus your efforts: By having a clear plan and strategy in place, you'll be better equipped to focus your efforts on the channels and platforms that are most appropriate for your target audience.

It helps you achieve your business goals: By aligning your content marketing strategy with your business goals, you'll be better equipped to achieve the results you're looking for.

It helps you measure your results: A content marketing strategy will also help you measure your results and determine what's working and what's not. This, in turn, will help you adjust your strategy as needed to ensure that you're achieving your business goals and resonating with your target audience.

Creating a strong content marketing strategy is a critical step in your content marketing efforts. By defining your business goals, understanding your target audience's pain points and needs, and choosing the right channels and platforms, you'll be better equipped to create content that resonates with your target audience and meets your business goals. In the following chapters, we'll dive deeper into the various platforms and channels for content marketing and discuss how to create effective and engaging content marketing campaigns on social media.

CHAPTER SIX

CHAPTER 4: CRAFTING ENGAGING AND EFFECTIVE SOCIAL MEDIA CONTENT

Social media has become a powerful tool for content marketing. With billions of people using social media every day, it provides a huge audience for your content and an opportunity to reach and engage with your target audience.

In this chapter, we'll discuss how to craft engaging and effective social media content that resonates with your target audience and supports your business goals.

Steps for Crafting Engaging and Effective Social Media Content

Know your audience: Before you start creating social media content, it's important to have a deep understanding of your target audience and what they want to see on social media.

Choose the right social media platforms: Based on your target audience, choose the social media platforms that are most appropriate for your audience.

Define your voice and tone: Define your brand voice and tone that you'll use on social media. This should align with your brand personality and resonate with your target audience.

Create visually appealing content: Use high-quality images, videos, and graphics to make your content visually appealing. This will help your content stand out on social media and attract the attention of your target audience.

Use a call to action: Encourage your target audience to take action by including a call to action in your social media content. This could be anything from asking them to like or share your post, to visiting your website or making a purchase.

Make use of trending topics and hashtags: Stay up-to-date on the latest trends and topics related to your industry and incorporate them into your social media content. This will help you reach a wider audience and increase engagement with your content.

Monitor and adjust: Finally, monitor the performance of your social media content and adjust your strategy as needed. This could include experimenting with different types of content, changing your tone and voice, or testing different calls to action.

Why Engaging and Effective Social Media Content Matters

It helps you reach a wider audience: Social media provides a huge audience for your content and an opportunity to reach and engage with your target audience.

It helps you build relationships with your audience: By creating engaging and effective social media content, you'll be able to build relationships with your target audience and establish your brand as a trusted and reliable source of information.

It helps you increase engagement: Engaging and effective social media content is more likely to be shared and interacted with by your target audience, which will help you increase engagement and reach a wider audience.

Crafting engaging and effective social media content is an important part of your content marketing strategy. By having a deep understanding of your target audience, choosing the right social media platforms, and creating visually appealing content with a strong call to action, you'll be better equipped to reach and engage with your target audience and achieve your business goals.

In the next chapter, we'll dive deeper into how to create and distribute video content on social media, and how to use video to engage with your target audience and achieve your business goals.

CHAPTER SEVEN

Chapter 5: Leveraging Influencer Marketing on Social Media

Influencer marketing has become an increasingly popular and effective way to reach and engage with your target audience on social media. Influencer marketing involves partnering with social media influencers to promote your brand and reach their followers.

In this chapter, we'll discuss how to leverage influencer marketing on social media to reach your target audience and achieve your business goals.

Steps for Leveraging Influencer Marketing on Social Media

Define your target audience: Before you start working with influencers, it's important to have a deep understanding of your target audience and what they want to see on social media.

Identify influencers in your industry: Look for influencers in your industry that have a large and engaged following that aligns with your target audience.

Evaluate influencer fit: Evaluate the fit between each influencer and your brand to ensure that they are a good match.

Establish a clear agreement: Establish a clear agreement with each influencer regarding the terms of your partnership, including the type of content they will create and share, the length of the partnership, and any compensation or incentives.

Monitor and adjust: Monitor the performance of your influencer marketing campaign and adjust your strategy as needed. This could include adjusting the type of content the influencer is creating and sharing, or working with a different influencer if the partnership is not working out.

Why Leveraging Influencer Marketing on Social Media Matters

It helps you reach a wider audience: By partnering with influencers, you'll be able to reach their followers and increase your brand's visibility on social media.

It helps you build trust with your target audience: Influencer marketing is a great way to build trust with your target audience by demonstrating that your brand is trusted by others.

It helps you increase engagement: Influencer marketing can help you increase engagement with your content on social media, which will help you reach a wider audience and build relationships with your target audience.

Leveraging influencer marketing on social media is a powerful way to reach and engage with your target audience and achieve your business goals. By identifying influencers that align with your target audience, establishing a clear agreement with each influencer, and monitoring the performance of your influencer marketing campaign, you'll be better equipped to reach and engage with your target audience and achieve your business goals.

In the next chapter, we'll explore how to use social media advertising to reach your target audience and achieve your business goals.

CHAPTER EIGHT

Chapter 6: Utilizing Social Media Advertising

Social media advertising is a great way to reach your target audience and achieve your business goals on social media platforms such as Facebook, Instagram, Twitter, and LinkedIn. In this chapter, we'll discuss the different types of social media advertising, the benefits of using social media advertising, and how to get started with social media advertising.

Types of Social Media Advertising

Boosted Posts: Boosted posts are regular posts on social media platforms that are promoted to reach a wider audience. Boosted posts can be used to increase the visibility of your content and reach your target audience.

Sponsored Posts: Sponsored posts are posts that are created and paid for by advertisers to reach a wider audience on social media platforms. Sponsored posts can be used to promote products, services, or events and reach your target audience.

Sponsored Stories: Sponsored stories are posts that appear in the news feed of a user's friends on social media platforms. Sponsored stories are a great way to reach a wider audience and increase the visibility of your content on social media.

Display Ads: Display ads are graphical ads that appear on the side or in-between content on social media platforms. Display ads are a great way to reach your target audience and increase the visibility of your content on social media.

Video Ads: Video ads are short video advertisements that appear in the news feed or in-between content on social media platforms. Video ads are a great way to reach your target audience and engage with them through visual content.

Benefits of Using Social Media Advertising

Reaches a Wider Audience: Social media advertising allows you to reach a wider audience on social media platforms, which is particularly useful if you are looking to reach a specific target audience.

Increases Visibility: Social media advertising increases the visibility of your content and helps you reach your target audience more effectively.

Increases Engagement: Social media advertising can help increase engagement with your content, which is important for building relationships with your target audience and achieving your business goals.

Offers Targeting Options: Social media advertising platforms offer a range of targeting options, including demographic targeting, location targeting, interest targeting, and more. This allows you to reach your target audience more effectively and achieve your business goals.

Offers Budget Flexibility: Social media advertising platforms offer budget flexibility, allowing you to set a budget that works for you and your business.

Getting Started with Social Media Advertising

Set your Goals: Before you get started with social media advertising, it's important to set clear goals for what you want to achieve with your advertising campaign. This could include increasing brand awareness, driving traffic to your website, or generating leads.

Define your Target Audience: Define your target audience and create a buyer persona to better understand their needs and wants. This will help you target your advertising efforts more effectively.

Choose the Right Platforms: Choose the right social media platforms for your advertising campaign, based on your target audience, budget, and business goals.

Create a Budget: Create a budget for your advertising campaign and allocate resources to different elements of your campaign, such as creating ads and monitoring results.

Test and Optimize: Test different advertising strategies and optimize your campaigns over time to improve results and achieve your business goals.

Social media advertising is a powerful way to reach your target audience and achieve your business goals on social media platforms. By understanding the different types of social media advertising, the benefits it offers, and how to get started with it, you can develop effective social media advertising campaigns that drive results for your business. When creating your campaigns, make sure to set clear goals, define your target audience, choose the right platforms, create a budget, and test and optimize your campaigns over time. With these steps in mind, you can take your content marketing efforts to the next level with social media advertising.

CHAPTER NINE

Chapter 7: Crafting Compelling Content for Social Media

Creating compelling content is key to engaging with your target audience on social media and achieving your business goals. In this chapter, we'll discuss the different types of content that can be used on social media, the elements of great content, and tips for creating content that resonates with your target audience.

Types of Content for Social Media

Images: Images are a great way to share information visually and engage with your target audience on social media. This can include photos of products, services, or events, as well as graphics, infographics, and more.

Videos: Videos are a powerful way to engage with your target audience on social media. This can include product demonstrations, how-to tutorials, behind-the-scenes looks, and more.

Blog Posts: Blog posts can be shared on social media to drive traffic to your website and provide more in-depth information about your products, services, or events.

Live Videos: Live videos are a great way to connect with your target audience in real-time on social media. This can include Q&A sessions, product demonstrations, and more.

Social Media Stories: Social media stories are short, ephemeral posts that disappear after 24 hours on platforms like Instagram and Snapchat. Stories are a great way to share behind-the-scenes content, daily updates, and more.

Elements of Great Content

Relevance: Content must be relevant to your target audience and their needs and interests.

Value: Content must provide value to your target audience, whether it be educational, entertaining, or both.

Authenticity: Content must be authentic and reflective of your brand's personality and values.

Consistency: Content must be consistent in terms of tone, style, and messaging, and align with your brand's overall content strategy.

Engagement: Content must encourage engagement with your target audience, whether through comments, shares, or other forms of interaction.

Tips for Creating Compelling Content

Know your Target Audience: Understanding your target audience and their needs and interests is key to creating content that resonates with them.

Plan your Content: Plan your content in advance and create a content calendar to ensure consistency and alignment with your overall content strategy.

Use Visuals: Visuals, such as images and videos, are an effective way to engage with your target audience on social media.

Be Authentic: Be authentic and reflective of your brand's personality and values in your content.

Encourage Engagement: Encourage engagement with your target audience by asking questions, including calls-to-action in your posts, and responding to comments and messages.

Crafting compelling content for social media is key to engaging with your target audience and achieving your business goals. By understanding the different types of content that can be used on social media, the elements of great content, and tips for creating content that resonates with your target audience, you can develop a strong content marketing strategy that drives results for your business on social media. So get creative, get strategic, and start crafting great content for your social media channels today!

CHAPTER TEN

Chapter 8: Measuring and Analyzing Social Media Success

To ensure that your social media marketing efforts are successful, it's important to measure and analyze your results on an ongoing basis. In this chapter, we'll discuss the different metrics you can use to measure your social media success, the importance of setting and tracking goals, and how to analyze your results to improve your social media marketing strategy.

Metrics to Measure Social Media Success

Engagement: Engagement metrics include likes, comments, shares, and other forms of interaction on your social media posts. Engagement metrics give you an indication of how well your content is resonating with your target audience.

Reach: Reach metrics measure the number of people who have seen your social media posts. Reach metrics can be used to measure the impact of your social media marketing efforts and determine whether you are reaching your target audience effectively.

Traffic: Traffic metrics measure the number of people who click on your social media posts and are directed to your website. Traffic metrics give you an indication of how effective your social media marketing efforts are at driving traffic to your website.

Conversion: Conversion metrics measure the number of people who take a desired action, such as making a purchase, signing up for a newsletter, or filling out a form, after clicking on your social media posts. Conversion metrics give you an indication of how effective your social media marketing efforts are at converting your target audience into customers or leads.

Setting and Tracking Goals

Before you begin measuring your social media success, it's important to set clear, measurable goals. This can include goals related to engagement, reach, traffic, conversion, or any other metric that is relevant to your business. Once you have set your goals, it's important to track your progress on an ongoing basis and adjust your social media marketing strategy as needed to achieve your goals.

Analyzing Your Results

Once you have set and tracked your goals, it's important to analyze your results to understand what is working well and what can be improved. This can include analyzing the performance of individual posts, the overall performance of your social media accounts, and the performance of your social media advertising campaigns. You can also use tools like Google Analytics to gain insights into the behavior of your target audience on your website and determine how they are interacting with your social media marketing efforts.

Measuring and analyzing your social media success is essential to ensuring that your social media marketing efforts are effective and achieving your desired results. By using the right metrics, setting and tracking goals, and analyzing your results, you can optimize your social media marketing strategy, improve your results, and drive success for your business on social media. So start measuring and analyzing your results today!

CHAPTER ELEVEN

Chapter 9: Leveraging User-Generated Content for Your Social Media Marketing

User-generated content (UGC) is a powerful tool for your social media marketing efforts. UGC refers to any content created by users of your social media platforms, such as comments, photos, videos, and reviews. In this chapter, we'll discuss the benefits of leveraging UGC for your social media marketing and how to encourage your followers to create and share UGC about your brand.

Benefits of Leveraging User-Generated Content

Increased Trust and Credibility: User-generated content is a form of social proof that can help build trust and credibility for your brand. By showcasing real experiences and opinions from your customers, you can provide potential customers with a more authentic and trustworthy view of your brand.

Improved Engagement: User-generated content is often more engaging than traditional marketing content. By encouraging your followers to create and share content about your brand, you can create a sense of community and foster deeper engagement with your audience.

Cost-Effective Marketing: User-generated content is often free or low-cost to create, making it a cost-effective way to add more content to your social media platforms. This is especially useful if you have a limited budget for marketing and advertising.

Targeted Reach: User-generated content is often shared among friends and followers, giving you the opportunity to reach a new, targeted audience. This can help you expand your reach and increase your visibility on social media.

Encouraging User-Generated Content

Run Contests and Giveaways: Running contests and giveaways on your social media platforms is a great way to encourage your followers to create and share UGC about your brand. Offer a prize for the best photo, video, or review about your brand and encourage your followers to share their entries with their own followers.

Use Hashtags: Encourage your followers to use a specific hashtag when sharing UGC about your brand. This will make it easier for you to track and curate the content and also help your brand become more discoverable on social media.

Highlight User-Generated Content: Showcase your favorite UGC on your social media platforms by reposting or sharing it with your own followers. This will not only help increase engagement with your own followers but also help build trust and credibility for your brand.

Provide Incentives: Offer incentives, such as discounts or exclusive access to products or events, to encourage your followers to create and share UGC about your brand.

Leveraging user-generated content can be a powerful tool for your social media marketing efforts. By taking advantage of the benefits of UGC and encouraging your followers to create and share content about your brand, you can improve engagement, build trust and credibility, and reach a targeted audience on social media. So start leveraging user-generated content today and see the benefits for yourself!

CHAPTER TWELVE

Chapter 10: Maximizing the Reach of Your Social Media Posts

Having a strong presence on social media is one thing, but getting your content seen by your target audience is another. In this chapter, we'll discuss ways to maximize the reach of your social media posts so you can get the most out of your social media marketing efforts.

Timing is Key: The timing of your social media posts is critical to maximizing their reach. Each social media platform has different peak times when users are most active, and posting during these times can increase your chances of getting more views and engagement. Research the peak times for your target audience on each platform and try to schedule your posts for these times.

Use Visuals: Visuals, such as images and videos, tend to perform better on social media than text-only posts. They are more eye-catching, memorable, and shareable. So make sure to include visuals in your social media posts to increase their reach and engagement.

Utilize Hashtags: Hashtags are a great way to increase the reach of your social media posts. By using relevant hashtags, you can make your posts more discoverable to users who are searching for related topics. Try to use a mix of popular, niche, and branded hashtags to reach a wider audience.

Engage with Your Followers: Engaging with your followers on social media can increase the reach of your posts. Respond to comments, like and share their posts, and ask for their feedback. This can help increase the visibility of your posts and build stronger relationships with your followers.

Collaborate with Influencers and Other Brands: Collaborating with influencers and other brands can help increase the reach of your social media posts. Partnering with influencers or other brands in your industry can help you tap into their audience and reach a new, targeted audience.

Paid Social Media Advertising: Paid social media advertising is another way to maximize the reach of your posts. Platforms like Facebook and Instagram offer targeted advertising options that can help you reach your target audience and increase the visibility of your posts.

Analyze Your Results: Regularly analyze the results of your social media efforts to see what is working and what is not. Use analytics tools to track the performance of your posts and make changes as needed to maximize their reach.

Maximizing the reach of your social media posts is critical to the success of your social media marketing efforts. By timing your posts well, using visuals, utilizing hashtags, engaging with your followers, collaborating with others, using paid advertising, and analyzing your results, you can increase the reach and engagement of your social media posts and get the most out of your efforts.

CHAPTER THIRTEEN

Chapter 11: Measuring the Success of Your Social Media Marketing Efforts

Once you've implemented your social media marketing strategy and started posting content, it's important to measure the success of your efforts. This chapter will discuss how to measure the success of your social media marketing efforts so you can make informed decisions about how to optimize and improve your strategy.

Set Goals: Before you can measure the success of your social media marketing efforts, you need to set goals. This could include increasing engagement, growing your following, driving traffic to your website, or increasing sales. Make sure your goals are specific, measurable, achievable, relevant, and time-bound (SMART).

Track Engagement: Engagement is one of the key metrics to track when measuring the success of your social media marketing efforts. Engagement includes likes, comments, shares, and any other interactions with your posts. Tracking engagement will give you an idea of how your content is resonating with your audience and what types of content they prefer.

Monitor Followers: Another important metric to track is the growth of your following. Monitoring your followers will give you an idea of how your social media presence is growing and if you're attracting new, targeted followers.

Track Website Traffic: Social media can be a powerful tool for driving traffic to your website. Tracking website traffic from your social media accounts will give you an idea of how successful you're being in driving traffic and converting that traffic into sales.

Use Analytics Tools: There are many analytics tools available that can help you measure the success of your social media marketing efforts. Platforms like Facebook and Instagram have built-in analytics tools, while third-party tools like Hootsuite and Sprout Social can provide more in-depth analysis and insights. Make sure to use analytics tools to track your progress and make data-driven decisions.

Compare to Competitors: Another way to measure the success of your social media marketing efforts is by comparing your performance to that of your competitors. This can give you an idea of how you're performing in comparison to others in your industry and identify areas for improvement.

Ask for Feedback: Finally, don't be afraid to ask for feedback from your followers. This can be in the form of comments, surveys, or focus groups. Ask for feedback on what they like and dislike about your content and what they would like to see more of.

Measuring the success of your social media marketing efforts is critical to the optimization and improvement of your strategy. By setting goals, tracking engagement, monitoring followers, tracking website traffic, using analytics tools, comparing to competitors, and asking for feedback, you can make informed decisions and continually improve your social media marketing efforts.

CHAPTER FOURTEEN

Chapter 12: Best Practices for Social Media Marketing

As you dive deeper into social media marketing, it's important to stay up to date with the latest best practices. This chapter will discuss the best practices for social media marketing so you can get the most out of your efforts and maximize your results.

Be Authentic: Authenticity is key when it comes to social media marketing. Your followers want to see the real you, not just a polished brand. Be yourself and let your personality shine through in your posts. This will help build trust and credibility with your followers and make your content more engaging.

Post Consistently: Consistency is key when it comes to social media marketing. Make sure to post regularly and consistently so your followers know when to expect new content from you. It's also important to post at the right times to reach your target audience when they're most active on social media.

Utilize Visual Content: Visual content, such as images and videos, are more engaging and likely to be shared than text-based posts. Make sure to incorporate visual content into your social media marketing strategy and use eye-catching graphics, images, and videos to grab the attention of your followers.

Engage with Your Followers: Engagement is a two-way street. Make sure to engage with your followers by responding to comments and messages, and liking and sharing their posts. This will help build a strong relationship with your followers and keep them engaged with your content.

Stay Up to Date with the Latest Trends: Social media is constantly evolving, so it's important to stay up to date with the latest trends and features. Make sure to keep an eye on new updates and changes to social media platforms, and adjust your strategy accordingly.

Collaborate with Influencers and Brands: Collaborating with influencers and brands can help you reach a new, targeted audience and drive more engagement. Look for influencers and brands that align with your brand values and target audience, and reach out to them to explore potential collaborations.

Keep Your Tone Consistent: Make sure to keep your tone consistent across all your social media channels. Your tone should align with your brand personality and be consistent with your overall marketing message.

Know the Rules and Guidelines: Every social media platform has its own set of rules and guidelines, so make sure to familiarize yourself with them. This will help ensure that your content is in line with each platform's policies and prevent your account from being penalized.

Following the best practices for social media marketing is key to maximizing your results and getting the most out of your efforts. By being authentic, posting consistently, utilizing visual content, engaging with your followers, staying up to date with the latest trends, collaborating with influencers and brands, keeping your tone consistent, and knowing the rules and guidelines, you can ensure that your social media marketing strategy is effective and successful.

CHAPTER FIFTEEN

Chapter 13: Measuring Your Social Media Success

Measuring the success of your social media marketing efforts is crucial to determine whether your strategy is working and to make any necessary changes. This chapter will discuss the key metrics to track and how to measure your social media success.

Track Engagement: Engagement metrics such as likes, comments, shares, and followers are important indicators of how well your content is resonating with your audience. Keep track of these metrics and look for trends over time to see how your engagement is growing.

Monitor Reach: Reach is the number of unique users who have seen your content. Monitoring your reach will help you understand how far your content is spreading and whether you're reaching your target audience.

Measure Click-Through Rates: Click-through rates (CTR) are a key metric to track, as they indicate the number of people who are clicking on your content and taking action. Keep track of your CTRs and look for opportunities to increase them, such as optimizing your call-to-action or using more visually engaging content.

Analyze Conversion Rates: Conversion rates are the number of people who take a desired action after engaging with your content, such as making a purchase or signing up for your email list. Make sure to track your conversion rates and look for ways to increase them, such as improving your website or offering more valuable content.

Monitor Website Traffic: Your social media marketing efforts should drive traffic to your website, so it's important to monitor your website traffic to see how it's affected by your social media marketing. Look for trends in website traffic and see if there are any correlations with your social media engagement.

Use Social Media Analytics Tools: Social media analytics tools can provide detailed insights into your social media performance, such as which posts are performing best, who your audience is, and which channels are driving the most traffic. Use these tools to gain deeper insights into your social media marketing performance and make informed decisions about your strategy.

Set and Track Goals: Setting and tracking goals is key to measuring your social media success. Make sure to set realistic and attainable goals, and track your progress towards those goals over time. This will help you see what's working and what's not, and make any necessary adjustments to your strategy.

Measuring your social media success is an important part of any social media marketing strategy. By tracking engagement, reach, click-through rates, conversion rates, website traffic, using social media analytics tools, and setting and tracking goals, you can gain valuable insights into your social media performance and make informed decisions about your strategy. This will help you maximize your results and ensure that your social media marketing efforts are effective and successful.

CHAPTER SIXTEEN

Chapter 14: Staying Up-to-Date with Social Media Trends

Social media is a constantly evolving platform, and it's important to stay up-to-date with the latest trends and changes in order to remain effective in your social media marketing efforts. This chapter will discuss the importance of staying informed and offer tips on how to stay up-to-date with social media trends.

Follow Industry Leaders: Following industry leaders and influencers in the social media space can provide valuable insights into the latest trends and changes in the industry. Look for individuals who are knowledgeable and active on social media, and make sure to regularly read their blogs, articles, and social media posts.

Attend Conferences and Events: Attending conferences and events dedicated to social media can provide you with the opportunity to learn from experts, network with other professionals, and stay informed about the latest trends and changes in the industry.

Join Online Communities: Joining online communities such as forums, Facebook groups, and LinkedIn groups dedicated to social media marketing can provide valuable insights into the industry and help you stay up-to-date with the latest trends.

Keep an Eye on Social Media Platforms: Social media platforms are constantly changing and updating, so it's important to stay informed about any new features or changes. Make sure to regularly check the official blogs and news sections of the platforms you use, and be on the lookout for any updates or changes.

Read Industry Reports and Studies: Industry reports and studies can provide valuable insights into the state of social media and help you stay up-to-date with the latest trends and changes. Make sure to regularly read these reports and studies and look for insights that can be applied to your social media marketing strategy.

Stay Active on Social Media: By staying active on social media and regularly engaging with your audience, you can stay up-to-date with the latest trends and changes. This will help you stay in touch with your audience and be able to respond to any new trends or changes quickly and effectively.

Staying up-to-date with social media trends is an important part of any social media marketing strategy. By following industry leaders, attending conferences and events, joining online communities, keeping an eye on social media platforms, reading industry reports and studies, and staying active on social media, you can stay informed and remain effective in your social media marketing efforts. This will help you stay ahead of the curve and ensure that your social media marketing strategy is always effective and relevant.

CHAPTER SEVENTEEN

Chapter 15: Measurement and Analytics

Measuring the success of your social media marketing efforts is crucial in determining whether your strategy is working and making the necessary adjustments. This chapter will discuss the importance of measuring and analyzing your social media efforts, and offer tips on how to effectively track and measure your results.

Define Your Goals: Before you can measure your results, it's important to define what success looks like for your social media marketing efforts. This includes setting specific, measurable, attainable, relevant, and time-bound (SMART) goals that align with your overall marketing strategy.

Use Built-In Analytics Tools: Most social media platforms offer built-in analytics tools that provide valuable insights into your social media performance. Make sure to regularly check these tools and use the data to adjust your strategy and improve your results.

Track Engagement Metrics: Engagement metrics, such as likes, comments, and shares, provide valuable insights into how your audience is responding to your content. By regularly tracking these metrics, you can measure the success of your content and make adjustments as needed.

Monitor Your Followers: Keeping an eye on your followers can provide valuable insights into the growth of your social media presence. Track the number of followers you have on each platform, and look for trends and changes in your audience over time.

Track Website Traffic: Tracking website traffic from social media can provide valuable insights into the success of your social media marketing efforts. Make sure to use tools such as Google Analytics to track website traffic from social media, and look for patterns and trends over time.

Monitor Competitors: Monitoring your competitors can provide valuable insights into the industry and help you stay ahead of the curve. Use tools such as social listening and competitive analysis to keep track of your competitors' social media efforts and look for areas where you can improve.

Regularly Review and Analyze: Regularly reviewing and analyzing your social media results is crucial in determining the success of your efforts. Make sure to regularly check your metrics and look for trends and patterns over time. Use this data to make adjustments to your strategy and improve your results.

Measurement and analytics play a critical role in determining the success of your social media marketing efforts. By setting SMART goals, using built-in analytics tools, tracking engagement metrics, monitoring followers, tracking website traffic, monitoring competitors, and regularly reviewing and analyzing your results, you can effectively track and measure the success of your social media marketing efforts. This will help you make informed decisions, adjust your strategy as needed, and ultimately achieve better results from your social media marketing efforts.

CHAPTER EIGHTEEN

Conclusion: Taking Your Content Marketing to the Next Level

In this book, we've explored the basics of social media content marketing and provided tips on how to effectively create and share content that engages and resonates with your audience. By following the tips outlined in this book, you can improve your social media presence, build brand awareness, and drive business results.

However, the social media landscape is constantly evolving, and staying ahead of the curve requires continuous learning and adaptation. To take your content marketing to the next level, consider the following steps:

Stay Up-to-Date on Industry Trends: Stay informed about the latest social media trends and best practices to ensure your content marketing strategies are relevant and effective. Attend industry events, read relevant blogs and articles, and follow influencers in your industry to stay up-to-date on the latest developments.

Experiment and Innovate: Don't be afraid to experiment with new tactics and strategies. Try new formats, such as live videos, or incorporate emerging technologies, such as augmented reality, into your content marketing.

Collaborate with Other Brands: Collaborating with other brands can help you reach a new audience, gain valuable insights, and generate new ideas for content. Look for opportunities to collaborate with complementary brands, influencers, and industry leaders.

Measure and Analyze Your Results: Regularly measuring and analyzing your results is essential in determining the success of your content marketing efforts. Use tools such as analytics and customer feedback to gain valuable insights into your audience and make informed decisions about your strategy.

Stay Authentic: Above all, stay true to your brand and audience. Authenticity is critical in building trust and engagement with your audience, so always strive to create content that is true to your brand and resonates with your audience.

By staying up-to-date on industry trends, experimenting and innovating, collaborating with other brands, measuring and analyzing your results, and staying authentic, you can take your content marketing to the next level. These steps will help you create impactful, effective, and engaging content that drives results for your business.

social media content marketing is an essential component of a successful marketing strategy. By following the tips outlined in this book, you can improve your social media presence, build brand awareness, and drive business results. Remember, the key to success is to stay informed, experiment, collaborate, measure, and always stay true to your brand and audience. Happy content marketing!

Printed by Libri Plureos GmbH in Hamburg,
Germany